Patrick Chalmers, John Francis

Mr. John Francis of the Athenaeum

On the Plan of Sir Rowland Hill

Patrick Chalmers, John Francis

Mr. John Francis of the Athenaeum
On the Plan of Sir Rowland Hill

ISBN/EAN: 9783743316577

Manufactured in Europe, USA, Canada, Australia, Japa

Cover: Foto ©ninafisch / pixelio.de

Manufactured and distributed by brebook publishing software
(www.brebook.com)

Patrick Chalmers, John Francis

Mr. John Francis of the Athenaeum

WIMBLEDON,

January, 1889.

SIR,

The Pamphlet herewith contains a fresh and most valuable contribution in proof of my contention that the Adhesive Postage Stamp, which saved and has carried out in practice the Reformed Postal System of 1810, formed no part of the proposals or intentions of Sir ROWLAND HILL, the merit of which has been usurped by him from JAMES CHALMERS, of Dundee.

I now ask you to read the record left on this subject by no less a man than the late Mr. JOHN FRANCIS, of the *Athenæum*, and friend of Sir ROWLAND HILL.

The Appendix gives a condensed account of the wide recognition now obtained in favour of JAMES CHALMERS, not only in this country, but throughout the United States of America and in the chief cities of the Continent.

Yours respectfully,

PATRICK CHALMERS.

MR. JOHN FRANCIS,

OF THE *ATHENÆUM*,

ON

The Plan of Sir Rowland Hill.

BY

PATRICK CHALMERS,

FELLOW OF THE ROYAL HISTORICAL SOCIETY.

SECOND EDITION.

LONDON:

EFFINGHAM WILSON & CO., ROYAL EXCHANGE, E.C.

1889.

MR. JOHN FRANCIS,

of the "Athenæum,"

On the Plan of Sir Rowland Hill.

FEW readers will require to be told that the late Mr. John Francis, whose testimony I am now about to bring forward in support of my case on the subject of the Adhesive Postage Stamp, was a leading man in the literary circles of London. Born in 1811, he became engaged on the staff of the *Athenæum* in 1831, ultimately rising to be chief of that great literary journal until the period of his death in 1882. In all the reforms of that period tending to remove the shackles from the Press and to advance the cause of education and learning, Mr. Francis took a prominent part, more especially in advocating such measures as the abolition of the "Taxes on Knowledge," and in promoting the Penny Postage Reform brought forward by the then Mr. Rowland Hill. A work in two volumes, entitled "John Francis, Publisher of the *Athenæum*: a Literary Chronicle of Half a Century," compiled by his son, Mr. John C. Francis, has lately been published, in which the names of most of the prominent writers and public men during the period throughout which his own labours extended are brought forward, with some account of their proposals and the benefits resulting from their efforts.

The warm interest which Mr. Francis took in the proposed Penny Postage Scheme of 1837 brought him into close relationship with Mr. Rowland Hill, an intimacy or indeed friendship which continued throughout their respective lives. What Mr. Francis has to say on this subject is consequently of much importance to all readers of this Chalmers-Hill controversy. Here, then, is the testimony of Mr. Francis as respects the plan proposed by Mr. Rowland Hill for carrying out the Penny Postage Scheme in practice :—

"On the 6th May, 1837, the *Athenæum* gave a short
" notice of Rowland Hill's pamphlet ' Post Office Reform,'
" and expressed its conviction that his statements and
" reasoning were worthy of the most serious consideration,
" though hesitating to acquiesce entirely in his conclu-
" sions. On the 21st and 28th April, 1838, it returns to
" the question in two leading articles upon the ' Minutes of
" Evidence taken before the Select Committee on Postage,'
" the Committee having been appointed for the purpose of
" examining the mode recommended by Rowland Hill for
" charging and collecting postage. The writer of the
" article says :—' The facts made known by this Report
" excite in us some astonishment. . . . 1,000 letters
" can be conveyed to Edinburgh or Dundee for one
" shilling, and within forty-eight hours, and the postage
" charge for delivery is 1s. 1½d. ! Mr. Hill proposed the
" issue of penny stamped covers for letters. Having seen
" that the Chairman of Stamps and Taxes mentions a
" ' peculiar paper with lines of thread or silk stretched
" through its substance, which is the best preventative of
" forgery he has seen,' and therefore likely to prevent
" these stamped covers from being forged, we have
" requested Mr. Dickenson, the inventor, to manufacture
" for our next number so much of this threaded paper as
" shall be sufficient for our whole impression, which will
" be printed upon it so as to make our subscribers
" acquainted with the nature of the proposed method.'
" The issue of April 28th (1838) had these blue threads
" inserted in the substance of the paper, and the article
" states—' We shall be surprised if so simple a means of
" protecting the revenue and preventing crime is not
" adopted.' "

Such is the record of Mr. Francis, the friend of Sir Rowland Hill. The scheme of 1837 is first commented on in May of that year. Attention is continued and directed to all that took place up to the proceedings of the House of Commons Select Committee in the following year, and then in April, 1838, we have two articles on the subject. On the 21st April Mr. Francis' great journal "returns to the question," telling us that "Mr. Hill proposed the issue of penny stamped covers for letters," mentions the way in which it was proposed to get over the difficulty of forgery by the use of Dickenson's "peculiar paper," and in its next issue of the 28th April actually prints that issue upon this same "peculiar paper," in order to show the public the manner in which Mr. Hill's scheme was to be carried out in practice. Not a word or a whisper does Mr. Francis utter as to an Adhesive Stamp having either been proposed or being for one moment contemplated, altogether exactly confirming my own account of the matter, and which account I desire here to repeat so that the same may be compared with this record left us by this learned and intimate acquaintance of Sir Rowland Hill and his proposals.

From "THE ADHESIVE POSTAGE STAMP, 1886."

"The plan by which Mr. Rowland Hill, in his pamphlet of 1837, proposed to carry out in practice his uniform penny postage scheme was, shortly stated, first, simply to pay the penny or money with the letters; but secondly, and more especially, by stamped sheets of letter paper, and stamped wrappers or covers. 'Let stamped covers and sheets of 'paper be supplied to the public, from the Stamp Office or 'Post Office, or both, and at such a price as to include the 'postage.' . . . 'Economy and the public convenience 'would require that sheets of letter paper of every descrip-'tion should be stamped on the part used for the address; 'that wrappers, such as are used for newspapers, as well as

' covers made of cheap paper, should also be stamped,' and
kept on sale at the post-offices. ' Stationers would also be
' induced to keep them.'

" What Mr. Hill overlooked in this proposal, was the
broad fact that he sets up the Stamp Office or Post Office to
do the business in letter paper of the stationers throughout the kingdom—some huge Government establishment
against which competition would be hopeless, as the Stamp
Office was to sell the writing paper at cost price, while the
stationer requires a profit to pay his rent and expenses, and
to live upon. The effect upon the stationers, consequently,
would have been confiscation—and against this plan the
united body of paper makers and stationers subsequently
protested.

" The Select Committee of the House of Commons of
1837-38, again, took exception to Mr. Hill's plan mainly on
account of its liability to forgery—a stamp of the nature
proposed would be extensively forged. After evidence on
the part of the Stamp Office authorities and papermakers
had been taken, it was decided to recommend that the
paper for all stamped covers should be manufactured at
the paper-mills of a Mr. Dickenson, or of another, solely,
under strict excise supervision. This paper of Mr. Dickenson's was of a peculiar make, having threads of cotton or
silk so interwoven in the paper that a post-office clerk could
readily know by the look or feel that a stamped cover was
genuine. The papermakers protested and petitioned
against this, objecting to one of the body having all the
work. Besides, the proposal involved permanent excise
supervision over the manufacture of paper. This proposal,
however, extended only to covers or envelopes ; how forgery
was to be prevented in respect to the stamps upon the
sheets of letter paper the Committee do not say. The
whole position, in fact, remained in a state of chaos, only
relieved by the ultimate adoption of the adhesive stamp,
which plan Mr. Chalmers had laid before this Committee
through Mr. Wallace, the Chairman, and likewise through
Mr. Chalmers, M.P., a member of the Committee, and

which plan had been publicly discussed, not without find-
ing adherents, including Mr. Cobden, one of the witnesses
in favour of the scheme.

" To the solution proposed by the Committee that all
stamped covers should be made of Dickenson's peculiar
paper the Government again highly objected, further adding
to the dilemma ; and when the Chancellor of the Exchequer,
on the 5th of July, 1839, introduced and carried a resolution sanctioning a Penny Postage Bill being brought forward, he distinctly only ' asked Hon. Members to commit
' themselves to the question of a uniform rate of postage of
' one penny at and under a weight hereafter to be fixed.'
Everything else was to be left open. ' If it were to go forth
' to the public to-morrow morning that the Government had
' proposed, and the House had adopted, the plan of Mr.
' Rowland Hill, the necessary result would be to spread
' a conviction abroad that, as a stamped cover was
' absolutely to be used in all cases, which stamped covers
' were to be made by one single manufacturer, alarm would
' be felt lest a monopoly would thereby be created, to the
' serious detriment of other members of a most useful and
' important trade. The sense of injustice excited by this
' would necessarily be extreme. I therefore do not call
' upon the House either to affirm or to negative any such
' proposition at the present. I ask you simply to affirm
' the adoption of a uniform penny postage, and the taxation
' of that postage by weight. Neither do I ask you to pledge
' yourselves to the prepayment of letters, for I am of
' opinion that, at all events, there should be an option of
' putting letters into the post without a stamp.

" ' If the resolution be affirmed, and the Bill has to be
' proposed, it will hereafter require very great care and
' complicated arrangements to carry the plan into practical
' effect. It may involve considerable expense and con-
' siderable responsibility on the part of the Government ;
' it may disturb existing trades, such as the paper trade.'
' .   .   .   ' The new postage will be distinctly and simply
' a penny postage by weight.'   .   .   .   ' I also require for

' the Treasury a power of taking the postage by anticipation,
' and a power of allowing such postage to be taken by
' means of stamped covers, and I also require the authority
' of rating the postage according to weight.' " *

" In this dilemma, as to *how* to carry out the scheme in
practice, Mr. Wallace favourably suggested the Adhesive
Stamp, the adoption of which plan, he had no hesitation in
saying from the evidence adduced, would secure the revenue
from loss by forgery. Mr. Warburton, also a member of
the 1837–38 Committee, ' viewing with considerable alarm
' the doubt which had been expressed of adopting Mr. Hill's
' plan of prepayment and collection by stamped covers,'
recommended that plans should be applied for from the
public.

" Again, in the House of Lords on the 5th of August,
Lord Melbourne, in introducing the Bill, is as much em-
barrassed as was the Chancellor of the Exchequer in the
Commons. The opponents of the Bill use, as one of their
strongest arguments, the impossibility of carrying out the
scheme in practice. The Earl of Ripon says :—' Why
' were their Lordships thus called upon at this period of
' the session to pass a Bill, when no mortal being at that
' moment had the remotest conception of how it was to be
' carried into execution ? ' Here Lord Ashburton, like Mr.
Wallace in the Commons, favourably suggested the Adhesive Stamp, ' which would answer every purpose, and
' remove the objection of the stationers and papermakers
' to the measure.'

" Let it, then, be clearly noted that, up to the period of
the Bill in July and August, 1839, not a word is said in
any way connecting Mr. Hill's name with other than the
impressed stamp on the sheet of letter paper, or, more especially, on the stamped covers. That, *and that alone*, is
taken on the one part as *his* plan by all the speakers,
official or otherwise—for that alone does the Chancellor of
the Exchequer ask for ' powers.' The Adhesive Stamp is

* See ' Hansard," Vol. 48.

brought in, on the other part, as a distinct proposal, in no way entering into the proposals of Mr. Hill."

Now, what does Sir Rowland Hill tell us of all this in his "History of Penny Postage"? Not a word! giving his readers, on the contrary, to understand that the adoption of the Adhesive Stamp was included in his proposals of 1837. I give another extract from one of my pamphlets commenting on this as under :—

"Let me here ask the reader's attention for a moment to that scene in the House of Commons on the 5th July, 1839, and on a subsequent occasion in the House of Lords. Here was a Bill on which the nation had set its heart—the prospect of a uniform penny postage had been brought within measurable distance of completion, but yet wanted the motive power. Ministers and Members of the Legislature alike were at fault as to *how* to carry it out in practice, and the voice of the Opposition rose aloud in jeering tones, 'Why should we be called upon to pass this Bill 'when no mortal being had the remotest conception of 'how it was to be carried into execution?' Has not the man who solved that problem, who made that prospect a reality, yet himself unrewarded, neglected, and unknown,—has not that man deserved well of his country?

"Then what of the professed and reputed originator of all this—enriched in life, canonised in death—what does Sir Rowland Hill tell us of these memorable scenes, the struggle and crisis of the fight? What says he of them in that 'History of Penny Postage' written by himself for the information of his countrymen and posterity? Of the dilemma of the Government, the sneers of the Opposition, or the interposition of Mr. Wallace and Lord Ashburton, he tells us not a line, nor a word—all totally ignored. And why? *Because to have breathed a whisper of these matters of 1839 would have been ignominiously to extinguish his pretensions to a prior proposal of an adhesive stamp, or of any-*

thing approaching to such a proposal. Long years were allowed to elapse before a 'History' such as this was placed before the public—the facts would be forgotten—no man would arise to question the statements or pretensions of one who had clenched that public so thoroughly in his grasp. That he may be looked upon as an originator where he was only an adapter or copyist at the dictation of others, reference to matters of the most vital interest in the history of this reform is wholly omitted. Statements in Parliament of the first importance, and essential to the right understanding of this history the facts of which he has professed to set forth, are left wholly unnoticed. And for what purpose? To add to his own brow unmerited laurels, stripped from a helpless and deserving man; and leaving that man, upon whose brains he had flourished, despoiled of reward, and, as far as the spoiler cared, consigned to oblivion."

———————

The Bill passed into law on the 17th August, 1839, whereupon Mr. Hill was appointed to a position in the Treasury for the purpose of superintending its carrying out. The first step taken was to advertise for plans from the public, and nothing better having been found, the Adhesive Stamp was adopted by Treasury Minute of date 26th December, 1839, in conjunction with Mr. Hill's plan of stamped covers, or stamp impressed upon the sheet of letter paper itself.

This Treasury Minute, drawn up under the supervision of Mr. Rowland Hill himself, at length provides for both stamps, impressed and adhesive, "the paper to be peculiar in its water-mark or some other feature," or, as recited in the Act of Parliament, " which paper shall have such distinguishing words, letters, figures, marks, lines, threads, or other devices marked into or visible in the substance of same, as the said Commissioners of Excise shall from time to time order and direct."

It is now necessary to note the reception the respective

stamps met with from the public as described in the pages of the "Encyclopædia Britannica" and by Sir Rowland Hill himself:—

"Mulready's well-remembered allegorical cover came "into use on the 1st May, 1840, together with the first "form of the stamped letter-paper and the adhesive labels. "They all met at first, but only for a few days, with a "large sale. That of the first day yielded £2,500. Soon "afterwards, the public rejection of the 'Mulready "envelope,' writes Rowland Hill, 'was so complete as to "necessitate the destruction of nearly all the vast number "prepared for issue.' Whilst, on the other hand, the "presses of the Stamp Office were producing more than "half a million of adhesive labels by working both night "and day, they yet failed to meet the demand."

The Adhesive Stamp thus saved the penny postage scheme from failure, and it will now be interesting to note how completely, at a subsequent period, Mr. Rowland Hill recognises this fact, while wholly unable to recollect anything whatever about the "peculiar paper with lines of thread or silk stretched through its substance" recorded in the pages of Mr. Francis.

In March, 1852, Mr. Hill was examined before the Select Committee of the House of Commons on "Archer's Patent." For five years previously a Mr. Archer had pressed upon the Post Office, Stamp Office, and the Treasury, a plan for perforating the sheets of postage stamps in the manner we are now familiar with, the practice, up till then, having been to use scissors or a knife wherewith to separate the stamps. In vain, however, did Mr. Archer all this while press on the authorities this great improvement. Mr. Hill did not see much in it, though considering it "advisable," and the Treasury grudged Mr. Archer's terms. At length some Members of Parliament took up the proposal, and Mr. Muntz obtained a Select Committee to investigate the matter, resulting in a unanimous approval, and Mr. Archer got £4,000 for his invention.

Under examination before this Committee on the different systems of stamps, Mr. Hill first gives the members to understand that *he* was the original inventor or proposer of the Adhesive Postage Stamp :—

" *Question* 962 : I believe you are the original inventor, " or the proposer, of the Penny Postage Stamp ?—*Answer:* " *Yes.*" A statement, however, rather too much for the Committee, some of whom had been present in the House of Commons on that eventful night, already described, when all was dismay as to how the Penny Postage Bill was to be carried out. Had they not been officially told that Mr. Hill's plan was " that an impressed stamped cover was absolutely to be used in all cases ? " Did they not recollect that it was through the interposition of Mr. Wallace the Adhesive Stamp was then proposed and ultimately arrived at ? Mr. Hill, then, is subsequently asked :—

" *Question* 991 : The Committee of 1837-8, for inquiring " into the postage, do not appear to have entered to any " extent into the difficulty of forgery with those different " systems ?—*Answer* : I think not ; they took the opinion " of the Stamp Office, which was to the effect that practical " security against forgery could be obtained.

" *Question* 992 : Their principal hope as a preventive " of forgery was in adopting a distinctive sort of paper for " envelopes, was it not ?—*Answer* : *I cannot recollect.*" . . .

Such, then, was the Mr. Hill with whom the simple-minded provincial bookseller had to deal when laying his claim to the merit of the Adhesive Postage Stamp, that stamp which had saved the scheme while the covers had to be destroyed as useless. Mr. Hill unhesitatingly assures this Committee against all evidence and the knowledge of some of them that *he* was the originator of the former, but about the covers of the proposed " peculiar paper " he " cannot recollect." Some of the Committee could recollect all about this peculiar paper, Mr. Hill could not recollect— the covers had proved a failure, the Adhesive Stamp had saved the scheme—*that* was the plan to stick to, of the other the less said the better. His friend, Mr. Francis, however, well recollected and records the facts—not a word from him about an Adhesive Stamp, the merit of which Mr. Francis would have been the first to claim for Rowland Hill had there been the smallest foundation for so doing—the impressed stamped cover was the plan of Mr. Hill, he tells us, the covers to be made of this "peculiar paper" on the recommendation of the authorities, and he had an issue of the *Athenæum* printed on that very paper to emphasise the fact and explain it to the public. A copy of this issue may now be seen, as I have just seen it, in the library of the British Museum, having these blue threads run through the paper. Was not Mr. Hill one of the very first to whom a copy of that issue was sent or shown? "There, Mr. Hill, you see, is your plan on the sort of paper your covers are to be made of"—yet now, the covers having been a failure, Mr. Hill "cannot recollect." Look also at the terms of the Treasury Minute of 26th December, 1839, already named—*Mr. Hill's own Minute*—requiring the very safeguard of a paper to be peculiar in its texture, anything as to which Mr. Hill cannot now remember, though he has no difficulty in assuring the Committee that he was the originator of the successful stamp, an assurance which a perusal of the proceedings in Parliament on the introduction of the Penny Postage Bill proves to be contrary to the fact and scatters to the winds.

But no second party was to be allowed by Mr. Rowland Hill to share with him the merit of this great reform, and just as he has succeeded in obtaining the credit of having *invented* the penny postage scheme itself—a scheme which investigation now shows to have been from beginning to end only a compilation of the prior proposals of others *

* Extract from Treasury Minute, of date 11th March, 1864, conferring upon Sir Rowland Hill, upon his retirement from active service, his full salary of £2,000 a year.

"My Lords do not forget that it has been by the powerful agency of the "railway system that these results have been rendered practicable. Neither "do they enter into the question, as foreign to the occasion, what honour "may be due to those who, *before the development of the plans of Sir Rowland* "*Hill, urged the adoption of Uniform Penny Postage.*"

—so has he usurped from James Chalmers the merit of the Adhesive Postage Stamp which saved it and has carried it out in practice.

To the above official and conclusive evidence that up to the introduction of the Penny Postage Bill in July, 1839, Mr. Rowland Hill had *not* proposed the adoption of the Adhesive Stamp, may be added further evidence to the same effect :—

First, when writing to James Chalmers under date 3rd March, 1838, acknowledging the plan of the Adhesive Stamp from Mr. Chalmers, Mr. Rowland Hill makes no pretension to having already proposed or being then in favour of an Adhesive Stamp. This is known from Mr. Chalmers having subsequently sent Mr. Hill a copy of that letter for the purpose of pointing out that fact to Mr. Hill. This correspondence, however, Mr. Rowland Hill removed from the Treasury, and same is now in the possession of Mr. Pearson Hill, who has not consented to produce that letter of 3rd March, 1838, publishing only such portion of the correspondence as appears to tell in his own favour.

Again, it is enough to point to Mr. Hill's letters to the Postmaster-General, Lord Litchfield, in January, 1838, explaining and enforcing his penny postage scheme then before the public, in which not a word is said of an adhesive stamp. In these Mr. Hill states his plan to be :—" That " the payment should always be in advance. And to rid this " mode of payment of the trouble and risk which it would " otherwise entail on the sending of letters, as well as for " other important considerations, I propose that the post- " age be collected by the sale of stamped covers."

Again, take the Press of the period—this is what the *Times* produces under date 30th August, 1839, a fortnight *after* the passing of the Bill :—" The Penny Postage will " commence, we learn, on the 1st January next. It is " intended that stamped envelopes shall be sold at every " post-office, so that stationers and other shopkeepers may,

" as well as the public, supply themselves at a minute's " notice." Not a word as to an adhesive stamp being any part of Mr. Hill's plan or proposal, or provided for in the Bill.

And yet in his " History of Penny Postage," and notwithstanding all these proofs to the contrary, Sir Rowland Hill, keeping all these proofs to the contrary wholly out of view, actually gives his readers to understand that the adoption of the Adhesive Stamp formed part and parcel of his original proposals of 1837 !

JAMES CHALMERS.

It has long been known in Forfarshire and adjacent counties that the inventor and proposer of the Adhesive Postage Stamp, the man who supplied what may be termed the *engines* to the otherwise immovable craft of Penny Postage Reform, was James Chalmers, bookseller, Dundee. When—about 1845—the merchants of the City of London handed their cheque of £13,000 to Mr. Rowland Hill in acknowledgment of his services, the citizens of Dundee, then a town not a quarter of its present size or population, not to be behindhand in asserting the share of their towns-man in the work, got up also their subscription, and, as of late years I have learned, on the 1st January, 1846, in the Town Hall of Dundee, and in the presence of the Provost, bankers, and leading citizens, James Chalmers was pre-sented with a Testimonial in recognition of his having been the originator of the Adhesive Postage Stamp, and for other postal services. And when, upon the decease of Sir Rowland Hill in August, 1879, the London papers pro-ceeded to attribute to him the entire merit of the reformed postal system, immediate protest was entered by means of letters and articles in the Dundee Press, recalling and re-asserting the services of James Chalmers.

This stage of the matter drew my attention to the subject of which up till then I knew little or nothing, having left Dundee at an early age, about the year 1834, and passed much of the interval abroad. Any charge therefore as to my having unduly delayed bringing forward my claim on behalf of my father is a mistake. Equally is it a mistake to call same a *new* claim—it is, on the contrary, an acknowledged claim of long standing, if generally unknown at this day to a new generation. To further prove this—when thirty years ago Sir Bartle Frere introduced the Adhesive Stamp into Scinde, he knew perfectly well that James Chalmers was the inventor; his letter to which effect I have published. Again, an able writer in that popular magazine, the *Leisure Hour*, before ever having heard of me or my publications, in an article describing " A Day at the Post Office," and what had there been shown him, designates the Adhesive Stamp the " Chalmers Stamp"; he had "always understood Chalmers to have been the originator." Take another instance : In a congratulatory letter acknowledging my pamphlets Mr. W. A. Warner, Secretary to the National Philatelical Society of New York, writes, under date May 3rd, 1887 : " I see that your father was the inventor of the Adhesive Stamp, and not Sir Rowland Hill, which fact I have always upheld for the last sixteen years. . . . I firmly believe that James Chalmers was the inventor of this means of applying the stamp, and deserves to be honoured by all Philatelists throughout the world." These instances show how widespread beyond his own locality the belief in Chalmers has been prior to my coming forward for the purpose of extending that belief.

To be told, therefore, that this is a new claim I am setting up, that I am too late in doing so, and that the present generation will consequently have none of it, is unfounded and unfair.

This plan of an adhesive postage stamp was invented by Mr. Chalmers, a well-known postal reformer, in the month of August, 1834, as conclusively proved to the satisfaction, after special investigation, of the leading biographical works of the day, the " Encyclopædia Britannica " and the " Dictionary of National Biography," and to the equal satisfaction of numerous other authorities at home and abroad who have read the evidence. Sir Rowland Hill, in his " History of Penny Postage," has left it on record that up to this period an adhesive postage stamp was " undreamt of."

This evidence has been published by me in a pamphlet of date 1884, entitled " James Chalmers the Inventor of the Adhesive Stamp, not Sir Rowland Hill." There is not only the testimony of an entire community who publicly presented the Testimonial already named, but the specific testimony of individuals now or lately living as to the date when Chalmers got up his sheets of adhesive stamps on his premises. To repeat all this testimony would be to republish a pamphlet, copy of which is at the service of any reader, who will find that the witnesses include gentlemen of position in the town, with three of the workmen in the employment of Mr. Chalmers in 1834, and the son of a fourth. W. Whitelaw describes the whole process—the setting up of the forme with a number of stamps having a printed device—the printing of the sheets —the melting of the gum—the gumming the backs of the sheets—the drying and the pressing—are all described, and the date already named conclusively proved. Nor is the date in any way a matter of mere recollection, but proved by specific events in the career of the individuals; as, for instance, by Mr. Prain, for many years the well-known and respected teacher of Brechin, and now Manager of the local Savings Bank, who left Dundee in the autumn of 1834, and testifies to having been shown the adhesive stamp in existence in Mr. Chalmers' premises before he left. Mr. D. Maxwell, Manager of the Hull Town Waterworks, formerly an *employé* of Mr. Chalmers, handled the adhesive stamp sheets in the premises and took part in clipping same previous to the 1st November, 1834, the date of his indenture as apprentice to another business, that of an engineer. Further specific testimony has just appeared in the columns of the Dundee Press. Mr. George Hood, then at the same engineering business, testifies to having known and been told of this by his then fellow apprentice, D. Maxwell, confirming the date. Mr. John D. Wears, father of the well-known Philatelist, Mr. T. Martin Wears, of Rosemount, Dundee, writes to the Press referring to the above testimony and adding: "To all this I should like "to add my own testimony. Having settled in Dundee in "May, 1835, I distinctly remember being shown within a "year of that date the stamped slips by James Chalmers "himself, who explained to me the use he intended they "should be put to. I cannot fix the exact date, but I know "it was before Robert Nicoll, the poet, left Dundee in the "summer of 1836, as I was frequenting his circulating "library at the time. James Chalmers has all along been "regarded by old residents in Dundee as the inventor of "the adhesive stamp." Much confirmatory evidence in a general way is added in my pamphlet of 1884, and such might have been indefinitely multiplied.

Immediately on the assembling of the Select Committee of the House of Commons in November, 1837, appointed to consider the proposed Penny Postage Scheme of Mr. Rowland Hill, Mr. Chalmers sent in his plan of prepayment by adhesive postage stamp to two members of the Committee, Mr. Wallace the Chairman, and Mr. Chalmers, M.P. for the Montrose Burghs. The date of Mr. Wallace's letter acknowledging receipt of this communication from Mr. Chalmers is the 9th December, 1837 ; this we know from the portion of the correspondence published by Mr. Pearson Hill and is admitted by him.

Mr. Chalmers also sent his plan to Mr. Cole, secretary to the Mercantile Committee of the City of London, who has bequeathed same to the South Kensington Museum Library, thus enabling me to publish his plan in detail, as under :—

SIR HENRY COLE'S PAPERS AND THE ADHESIVE STAMP OF Mr. CHALMERS.

In his "Fifty Years of Public Life," lately published, Sir Henry Cole gives much information with respect to the Penny Postage reform, a boon with the obtaining and carrying out of which he was intimately associated—first as secretary to the Mercantile Committee of the City of London, and afterwards as coadjutor to Mr. Rowland Hill at the Treasury. "A General Collection of Postage " Papers," having reference to this reform, elucidating the efforts made by this Committee of London Merchants and Bankers during the year 1838–39, to obtain for the scheme the sanction of the Legislature, has been bequeathed by Sir Henry Cole, " to be given to the British Museum after " my death."* " The Mercantile Committee," he states, " was formed chiefly by the exertions of Mr. George Moffat "in the spring of 1838. Mr. Ashurst conducted the Parlia- " mentary Inquiry, and upon myself, as Secretary, devolved " the business of communicating with the public." This Committee formed the source and focus of the agitation which brought about the ultimate enactment of uniform Penny Postage. Money was freely subscribed, meetings were held, public bodies in the Provinces were urged to petition, Members of Parliament and Ministers were waited upon, and a special paper advocating the scheme, termed the " Post Circular," was issued and circulated gratis. Of these proceedings Mr. Cole was the guiding genius ; and, amongst other successes, over two thousand petitions to Parliament were obtained—labours which were ultimately crowned with success.

To Mr. Cole, then, it now turns out that Mr. Chalmers, in February, 1838, sent a copy of his plan of the adhesive stamp. Mr. Wallace and the House of Commons Com- mittee had already got it, but it is only now that the particulars of the plan have been brought to light—and in

---

* These papers are in the Art Library of the South Kensington Museum.

this "Collection of Postage Papers," Sir Henry Cole has indeed left a valuable legacy to me, and to all prepared to recognise the true originator of the adhesive postage stamp. These papers include a printed statement of Mr. Chalmers' plan, dated "4 Castle Street, Dundee, 8th Feburary, 1838," and which runs as follows :—

" *Remarks on various modes proposed for franking letters,*
" *under Mr. Rowland Hill's plan of Post Office Reform.*

" In suggesting any method of improvement, it is only " reasonable to expect that what are supposed to be its ad- " vantages over any existing system, or in opposition to " others that have been or may be proposed, will bo " explicitly stated.

" Therefore, if Mr. Hill's plan of a uniform rate of " postage, and that all postages are to be paid by those " sending letters *before* they are deposited in the respective " post-offices, become the law of the land, I conceive that " the most simple and economical mode of carrying out " such an arrangement would be by *slips* (postage stamps) " prepared somewhat similar to the specimens herewith " shown.

" With this view, and in the hope that Mr. Hill's plan " may soon be carried into operation, I would suggest " that sheets of stamped slips should be prepared at the " Stamp Office (on a paper made expressly for the purpose) " with a device on each for a die or cut resembling that on " newspapers; that the *sheets* so printed or stamped " should then be rubbed over with a strong solution of gum " or other adhesive substance, and (when thoroughly dry) " issued by the Stamp Office to town and country distribu- " tors, to stationers and others, for sale in sheets or singly, " under the same laws and restrictions now applicable to " those selling bill or receipt stamps, so as to prevent, as " far as practical, any fraud on the revenue.

" Merchants and others whose correspondence is exten- " sive could purchase these slips in quantities, cut them

" singly, and affix one to a letter by means of wetting the
" back of the slip with a sponge or brush, just with as
" much facility as applying a wafer."—Adding that the
stamp might answer both for stamp and wafer, especially in
the case of circulars—a suggestion which those who may
recollect the mode of folding universally practised before the
days of envelopes, will appreciate. Mr. Chalmers goes on
—" Others, requiring only one or two slips at a time, could
" purchase them along with sheets of paper at stationers'
" shops, the *weight* only regulating the rate of postage in
" all cases, so as a stamp may be affixed according to the
" scale determined on.

" Again, to prevent the possibility of these being used a
" *second time*, it should be made imperative on postmasters
" to put the post-office town stamp (as represented in one
" of the specimens) across the slip or postage stamp."

Mr. Chalmers then goes on to point out the advantages
to be derived from this plan, and to state objections to
Mr. Hill's plan of impressed stamped covers or envelopes,
or stamp impressed upon the sheet of letter paper itself.
At that period envelopes—being scarcely known, and never
used, as involving double postage—were a hand-made
article, heavy and expensive; objections which have disap-
peared with the abolition of the Excise duty on paper, and
the use of machinery. But how true were Mr. Chalmers'
objections *then*, may be gathered from the fact, as recorded
by Sir Rowland Hill in his " Life," that the large supply
provided of the first postage envelope, the " Mulready," had
actually *to be destroyed* as wholly unsuitable and unsale-
able, while the supply of adhesive stamps was with difficulty
brought up to the demand. The force and value of Mr.
Chalmers' objections to the stamp impressed upon the
sheet itself, are best exemplified by the fact that, though
ultimately sanctioned by the Treasury at the instance of
Mr. Hill, such plan never came into use. People bought
their own paper from the stationers, and not from the
Stamp Office, and applied the adhesive stamp as the weight
required. Mr. Chalmers concludes, " taking all these dis-

" advantages into consideration, the use of stamped slips
" is certainly the most preferable system; and, should
" others who take an interest in the proposed reform view
" the matter in the same light as I do, it remains for them
" to petition Parliament to have such carried into opera-
" tion."

This statement of Mr. Chalmers is printed on part of
an elongated sheet of paper. On the half not occupied by
the type are several specimens of a suggested stamp, about
an inch square, and with the words printed, " General
Postage—not exceeding half-an-ounce—One Penny." And
the same—" Not exceeding one ounce—Twopence." (It is
only of late years that a penny has franked one ounce in
weight.) A space divides each stamp for cutting off
singly,* and the back of the sheet is gummed over. One
of the specimens is stamped across with the post-mark,
" Dundee, 10th February, 1838," to exemplify what
Mr. Chalmers states should be done to prevent the stamp
being used a second time.

Here is a complete description of the principle of the
Adhesive Stamp as ultimately adopted by Mr. Hill at the
Treasury by Minute of 26th December, 1839, when he sent
Mr. Cole to Messrs. Bacon & Petch, the eminent engravers,
to provide a die and contract for the supply of stamps (see
Mr. Bacon's evidence, as already published by me), a plan
in use to the present day.

This description, as now brought to light under the
signature of Mr. Chalmers himself, fully confirms the
evidence with respect to the invention in August, 1834, as
given by his then *employés* yet living, W. Whitelaw and
others just mentioned.

It will now be asked, " Seeing how easily and conclusively
it has been proved that the adoption of the Adhesive Stamp

* The perforated sheets were not introduced until the year 1852. This
improvement was the invention of a Mr. Archer, for which he got the sum of
£4,000, as already mentioned.

for the purpose of carrying out his scheme in practice formed no part of the original proposals or intention of Mr. Hill, how comes it that James Chalmers did not receive the official credit for his invention and timely proposal to which he was entitled?" The explanation or excuse which Mr. Hill, in reply to Mr. Chalmers' claim, set up for attributing, after all, the entire merit to himself is this:— When under examination before the Commissioners of Post Office Inquiry, on the 13th February, 1837, a difficulty arose as to what was to be done in the case of a person unable to write taking an unstamped letter and a penny to a post office, a stamped cover being compulsory, no money accepted in prepayment. The penny would buy one of Mr. Hill's stamped wrappers or covers, but the cover would obliterate the address, and the person could not write. In such a case, and in such a case only, says Mr. Hill, " perhaps this difficulty may be obviated by using a bit of paper just large enough to bear the stamp and covered at the back by a glutinuous wash, which the bringer might by applying a little moisture attach to the back of the letter, so as to avoid the necessity of redirecting it." Going on at once, however, to withdraw the compulsion to use a stamp at all: " Better, at first at least, accept the penny in cash for penny letters, so that every stamp used might be *universally* the impressed stamp." The " person who could not write" had thus only to pay the penny, no " bit of gummed paper" being required. And this penny in cash was accepted up to the year 1855.

Here, then, was a momentary allusion to a bit of gummed paper, showing that Mr. Hill had heard of Chalmers' invention of 1834, but without seeing its value or proposing its adoption for the purpose of carrying out the scheme. February, 1837, was two years and a half after the proved invention of the Adhesive Stamp by Mr. Chalmers, one of the early postal reformers, " who held correspondence with the postal reformers of his day, both in and out of Parliament" ("Encyclopædia Britannica")—the correspondent, amongst others, of Messrs. Knight & Co., who published for Mr. Hill. However, in a letter of 18th January, 1840, Mr. Hill informs Mr. Chalmers that his claim cannot be admitted because he, Mr. Hill, had himself anticipated Mr. Chalmers' proposal of December, 1837, by having himself proposed the adoption of the Adhesive Stamp in February of the same year! A mere pretence and afterthought bred of the success which had attended the proposal of Chalmers. Mr. Hill, as has been proved, had utterly failed to see the value of the Adhesive Stamp in place of having proposed to adopt it up to the very period of the introduction of the Penny Postage Bill in July, 1839, a year and a half *after* the official proposal to that effect by James Chalmers. In reply, Mr. Chalmers pointed this out to Mr. Hill, handing him a copy of his, Mr. Hill's, letter to him of 3rd March, 1838. "Why " did you not tell me anything of this before? *There* is " a copy of your letter of 3rd March, 1838, when I sent " you my plan, in which no such pretension is put " forward. It is only now that I learn for the first time " that you had ever proposed or been in favour of an " adhesive stamp."

But much had happened in the interval betwixt Mr. Hill's two letters to Mr. Chalmers. The stamp not accepted by Mr. Hill in 1838, had become in 1840 the favourite of all opinions concerned, the adopted of the Treasury. It had saved the scheme. Mr. Chalmers must now be put aside, and so this afterthought, this far-fetched pretext, was hit upon for the purpose; and Mr. Hill being in despotic power, Chalmers had to give way, though in any case not the man to raise further discussion on the matter, it being, to him, sufficient satisfaction that the public had got his plan.

MR. PEARSON HILL.

Mr. Pearson Hill has at length made an attempt by the publication of a pamphlet, entitled "The Chalmers Craze Investigated," to make a stand against the success which has attended my efforts to vindicate the title of my late father to having been the originator of the Adhesive Postage Stamp. This pamphlet is chiefly remarkable for personalities, and for omitting to give just what is wanted to elucidate this controversy—namely, the letters of Mr. Rowland Hill to Mr. Chalmers of dates 3rd March, 1838, and 18th January, 1840 ; and this notwithstanding requests for their production. We are favoured with an "Extract" from a letter of Mr. Chalmers to Mr. Rowland Hill of date 18th May, 1840, purporting to show that Chalmers "honestly abandoned" his claim, but the facts having been obscured and misrepresented to him, Chalmers honestly abandoned nothing (see page 40), while I have had no difficulty in showing in my "Letter to the Dundee Burns Club: a Reply to Mr. Pearson Hill," pages 21-26, that this very "Extract" itself proves that Chalmers was "first in the field" in having proposed the adoption of the Adhesive Stamp. That Mr. Pearson Hill should still have withheld this long asked for correspondence in its entirety is simply an affront to the understanding of all who have followed this controversy, and virtually an abandonment of his case. No amount of sophistries or pages of vituperation of me will blind any impartial mind to that fact. Nor is any explanation given as to by what right and with what object Mr. Rowland Hill removed this official correspondence of 1840 from the Treasury.

Mr. Pearson Hill's pamphlet is further remarkable for now making no pretension as to the adhesive stamp having been primarily or specially the invention of Sir Rowland Hill; though why he has allowed it to be believed until now that such stamp *was* the special invention of his father, Mr. Pearson Hill does not say. He thinks this stamp must have occurred to "scores of people," and so it did *in October*, 1839, to just 49 people when the Treasury advertised for plans, James Chalmers having already brought it forward in December, 1837, and its merits having been publicly discussed all through the interval. The "Rowland Hill" delusion being at length dispelled, Mr. Pearson Hill's motto is, "Anybody but Chalmers," "scores of people." Further, though still of opinion that the adoption of the adhesive stamp for the purpose of carrying out the scheme was included in Mr. Rowland Hill's proposals of 1837, Mr. Pearson Hill does not attempt to explain why neither Parliament, nor the Government, nor the Press, nor, as we now find, Mr. John Francis, the intimate friend of Sir Rowland Hill, knew anything to that effect up to the introduction of the Penny Postage Bill in July, 1839, any allusion whatever to the proceedings on which occasion Mr. Pearson Hill, equally with Sir Rowland Hill, suppresses as being fatal to his pretension.

Having regard to the objection displayed by Mr. Pearson Hill to producing more than the mere " Extract " from the correspondence which purported to tell in his own favour, to the unfounded imputations against me and the personalities he has indulged in, and to his whole mode of conducting this controversy, I now desire to state, on the part of myself and friends, that we shall now be satisfied with nothing short of the production and perusal of the originals of this correspondence, and that we shall feel justified in declining to recognise as sufficient or to take cognizance of any further extract or copy Mr. Pearson Hill may publish or put forward in any quarter.

In justification of this, it may be instructive if I reproduce some specimens from Mr. Pearson Hill's pen. Here, for instance, is his letter to the publishers of the " Encyclopædia Britannica " :—

> " 50, Belsize Park,
> " London, N.W.,
> " 15th March, 1883.

" Gentlemen,

" As you are now issuing a new edition of your " ' Encyclopædia Britannica,' and as for years past a " Mr. Patrick Chalmers has persistently been making false " and groundless charges against my father, the late Sir " Rowland Hill, I think it well to send you the enclosed "printed documents for your information, as it is by no "means improbable that he may strive to get you to insert "some untrue statement when you deal with the question "of the Post Office and Postal Reform.

"I need hardly say that I shall be happy at any time "to submit to you the original documents which are in my "possession, which disprove the claims put forward in "behalf of Mr. James Chalmers of Dundee, if you would "desire to see them.

"Your statistical information about the Post Office, as "given in my copy of the Encyclopædia (the eighth edition), "is of course now much behindhand. I dare say you have "already on your staff of contributors some gentlemen well "able to supply you with fresh information; but should "you be in want of any such help, I feel sure that my "cousin, Mr. Lewin Hill, head of the statistical branch of "the Secretary's office, General Post Office, London, would "gladly undertake the work if you desired it.

"I am, Gentlemen,

"Your obedient servant,

"(Signed)   PEARSON HILL.

"Messrs. A. & C. Black,
    "Edinburgh."

Having been courteously afforded the opportunity of stating my own case as against that of Mr. Pearson Hill and all his "documents," the result was the decision in my favour—that "James Chalmers was the inventor of the Adhesive Postage Stamp in the month of August, 1834"; and that Sir Rowland Hill's allusion in February, 1837, to the use such a stamp might be put to in the exceptional case already mentioned was to an idea "suggested from without." In place of retiring with dignity, if with regret, Mr. Pearson Hill has gone on to find fault with the conductors of this standard work, to challenge a decision initiated by himself, and to sneer at my witnesses as only men in their dotage. He further gives his sanction to the persistent way in which I have been misrepresented in the Press as "claiming the Penny Postage *Scheme* for my father," thus rendering my claim too ridiculous to obtain attention. A cause that has to be supported by such means must be weak indeed. The following from my late pamphlet, "A Reply to Mr. Pearson Hill," further illustrates his mode of conducting this controversy:—

"In the absence of a 'case' we all know the not uncommon alternative, 'abuse the other side,' and this may appear to you the course I have been honoured with here. Every one who has followed my publications knows how gradually the facts and evidence have come to hand, or within my own knowledge, yet I am taken to task as having kept back statements, for not having early published my case full blown. Again, I am somehow held responsible for Press statements, with which I had nothing to do, or, I may say, not even seen. In this way are Mr. Pearson Hill's strictures, complaints, and cavillings mustered. So far does he forget himself as to imply that I have claimed for my father not only the Adhesive Stamp, but further, the merit of Archer's patent perforation, and the very Penny Postage Scheme itself! That throwing over 'poor Mr. Samuel Roberts,' I have put James Chalmers in his place. Going on with such choice remarks as that 'Probably before the jubilee of Penny Postage arrives some 'old people in Dundee or Bedlam will be discovered who 'can testify that Mr. James Chalmers also designed the 'General Post Office in St. Martin's-le-Grand, and that the 'Postal Telegraphs, Telephones, and the Parcel Post were 'all invented by Mr. James Chalmers in 1834, and 'communicated by him to his wondering friends and 'neighbours.' Referring to my being a Member of the Royal Historical Society leads to the remark, 'A man may 'as well be called a goose because he subscribes to a Goose 'Club,' — concluding, 'Surely if the Commissioners in

' Lunacy are in want of a promising case they might find
' one at Wimbledon admirably adapted to their hands.'

    " I refrain from adding by any words of mine to the
painful effect which such remarks will produce upon any
man of intelligence or sense of propriety."

APPENDIX.

RECOGNITION OF JAMES CHALMERS AT HOME AND ABROAD.

In former publications I have already given copies of numerous articles and notices in recognition of James Chalmers as having been the originator of the Adhesive Postage Stamp, including thirty of the London Press, with a fairly numerous body of the Provincial and Scottish papers, headed by the "Encyclopædia Britannica," and the "Dictionary of National Biography." Special mention should also be made of the Glasgow Post Office Magazine, "The Queen's Head," containing an able article in recognition of Chalmers, nearly 5,000 copies of which have been subscribed for by the *employés* of the various post-offices in the United Kingdom. This article has been favourably received, including reviews by Philatelic journals on the Continent and in the United States.

To now print in full the additional articles which have more lately been published, and continue to come forward, would extend this publication to quite a further 200 pages. For the present, consequently, I must content myself with a mere summary or indication of these valuable recognitions, first noticing those at home.

Former able supporters, such as the *City Press, Whitehall Review, Croydon Review, Metropolitan, Home and Colonial Mail, Sunday Times, Bric-a-Brac, Manchester Guardian, Brighouse Gazette,* and others, lose no opportunity of returning warmly to the subject. The *City Press* writes: "Is the man who at a critical moment, and unrewarded, supplied the motive power to the Penny Postage scheme, a power to this day indispensable to the commerce and revenues of the world, to be left unmentioned, while every possible occasion is availed of to laud the services of Sir Rowland Hill?" The *Whitehall Review* says: "As a matter of common justice and right, it only now remains for those who have so publicly recognised Sir Rowland Hill to now as publicly recognise and acknowledge James Chalmers."

Well may these writers ask for discrimination in the Press

when treating of the subject of Penny Postage Reform. No one denies the great services of Sir Rowland Hill, but in the indiscriminate panegyrics customary amongst modern writers it is overlooked that " originality of conception " formed no part of his merits or proposals, the official Treasury declaration to which effect I have already given (see *ante*, page 13), while the Sir Rowland Hill Mansion House Committee abandoned his pretensions to originality, as admitted by the change of inscription effected by them upon the City statue of Sir Rowland Hill, and by the correspondence betwixt myself and the Lord Mayor (the Chairman), which has been published.* Further than this, the late Mr. Fawcett, H.M. Postmaster-General, in his remarks upon the occasion of unveiling this City statue, made no claim whatever to the effect that the uniform Penny Postage Scheme was in any particular an invention or conception on the part of Sir Rowland Hill, simply claiming him as the man to whom we are indebted for " *having introduced* " that scheme.

Another feature overlooked by many in now pointing to the large revenue derived from the Post Office is that of the heavy loss entailed by the introduction of penny postage during the first twenty-three years of the change. The old system previous to 1840 produced a net revenue of £1,634,000, and not until the retirement of Sir Rowland Hill in 1864 did the revenue recover itself to an equal amount, the comparative loss in the interval having amounted to £14,000,000 sterling.

The great publishing firm of Messrs. Trübner & Co., in a late circular, state : " Sir Rowland Hill has got a statue for his advocacy of cheap postage, although he had not the remotest idea of how it could be *successfully* carried out ; but the intelligent Dundee bookseller, James Chalmers, who, by inventing the Adhesive Postage Stamp, rendered cheap postage possible, has had no such recognition;" going on to urge that some public memorial should be equally raised to the memory of Chalmers. Such memorials, however, are rather for men who have once for all made their mark and done with ; in the case of Chalmers, his work remains with us in our daily social and commercial avocations, and what is here wanted is that those thus paying daily tribute to his memory, by using his indispensable stamp,

* See " Concealment Unveiled : a Tale of the Mansion House."— Effingham, Wilson, & Co., Royal Exchange.

should know the name of its originator. This knowledge, notwithstanding the yet silence of many influential journals, is being rapidly spread. Other great publishing circulars now to be claimed in recognition are, the *Publisher's Circular* (Messrs. Sampson, Low & Co.), the *Bookseller*, and the *Stationery Trades Journal;* with additional London papers, the *Boy's Own Paper, Home Work, Society Herald, Chit-Chat*, the *Star.* The *Leeds Times, Salford Chronicle, Wednesbury Herald, Huddersfield Daily Examiner, Belfast Morning News, Greenock Herald,* may be added to former adherents. I am indebted to Mr. F. Graham Aylward, of Hereford, for valuable letters published by the *Hereford Times,* the *Reading Mercury,* and other papers. The *British Economist,* or *Scottish Bankers' Magazine,* of Edinburgh, has favoured me with the desired recognition; and I have received the following letter from the Right Hon. Sir Thomas Clark, Bart., Lord Provost of Edinburgh :—

" CITY CHAMBERS, EDINBURGH,

" *February 23rd*, 1888.

" DEAR SIR,

" I have received the papers you have sent me regarding your father's claim to be the originator of the Adhesive Stamp.

" The evidence is very conclusive, and as one who used long ago to have constant relations with your father, I rejoice at your success in establishing his claim.

" I am,

" Very truly yours,

" (*Signed*) THOMAS CLARK,

" *Lord Provost of Edinburgh.*"

In Arbroath, the birthplace of James Chalmers, a volume of much interest and erudition, entitled " Arbroath, Past and Present," compiled by Mr. McBain, banker, Arbroath, has lately been published. In this work a biographical notice of James Chalmers is given, from which I extract the following :—

" To James Chalmers, a native of Arbroath, is due the distinguished honour of being the inventor of the Adhesive Postage Stamp, which was not only the means of saving the Penny Postage Scheme of this country, but of conferring a lasting benefit on the commerce of the world. . . . This honour for a time was claimed for Sir Rowland Hill, but thanks to the untiring exertions of his son, Patrick Chalmers, of London,

James Chalmers' claim to the honour has been indisputably established, and is now universally admitted. The benefits which have accrued from this invention are incalculable, and to-day every civilised nation is still reaping the fruit of the inventive genius of this distinguished Arbroathian."

In Dundee, in a late publication entitled "The Roll of Eminent Burgesses of Dundee, 1513 to 1886." "published by order of the Provost, Magistrates, and Town Council," edited by a distinguished writer there, Mr. A. H. Millar, and entailing much labour and research, a lengthened article is given detailing the career of James Chalmers, in the course of which his services are brought forward in terms similar to the Arbroath article. The resolution of the Dundee Town Council, of date 3rd March, 1883, formally recording their townsman to have been the originator of the Adhesive Stamp, "that indispensable feature in the success of the reformed Penny Postage Scheme," is here again brought forward, and the work is in the hands of many Scottish noblemen, wealthy merchants, and the public.

Something more than newspaper recognitions may now be recorded. In Wednesbury, Staffordshire, not far from Kidderminster where a statue of Sir Rowland Hill has been erected, a paper was lately read by a literary gentleman, Mr. J. E. Ryder, at a meeting of the Springhead Mutual Improvement Society, entitled " A Monumental Mockery," alluding to the adjacent statue at Kidderminster. In this paper Mr. Ryder points out that Sir Rowland Hill invented nothing whatever, giving the prior sources from which he obtained the Penny Postage Scheme, and further recognising James Chalmers as the man to whom we owe the Adhesive Stamp which saved and has carried out that scheme. "A discussion followed, and the evidence and arguments adduced in the paper were found to have resulted in convincing those present of the justice of the claims set forth. Votes of thanks to the essayist and chairman terminated the meeting."

Again, in the important town of Sheffield, Mr. G. R. Vine, a local *savant* and philatelist, has read a paper entitled " The Postage Stamp ; or, the History of a Fascination," before the " Sheffield Literary and Philosophical Society," in which the services of James Chalmers are set forth, and " the honour, no mean one,' of having been the originator of the Adhesive Postage Stamp unhesitatingly ascribed to him. "The working out of a plan, based upon previous Parliamentary Reports, &c., of a low-priced postal rate is due in a general sense to Rowland Hill." Mr. Vine writes me: "When I delivered this paper there were present some old Sheffield Post Office reformers, notably the Brittains (one the late Mayor of Sheffield), Alderman Hobson, and others; but in the discussion which followed the delivery none of those present cared to dispute your claim." The well-known and influential paper, the *Sheffield Daily Telegraph*, has, some time ago, appeared in the list of my adherents.

I have already mentioned that four out of the five philatelic papers published in this country have recognised Chalmers. A new paper just come out in Liverpool, entitled *The Stamp Collector's Gazette*, contains the following: "How about the 'Chalmers-Hill controversy?' I have had correspondence with both, and have read pamphlets on both sides, and I am of opinion that Mr. Chalmers has the best of it. When abuse steps in, and a man questions the sanity and honour of his adversary, I think one may safely give the other side the benefit of the doubt, if any. But there is no doubt in this case that Mr. P. Chalmers has made his case clear."

Coming now to the recognitions of James Chalmers abroad, it is mainly to the pursuit of Philatelism or postage stamp collecting that I am indebted for the warm interest which has been taken in the fresh light I have thrown upon the origin of the Adhesive Stamp. In the United States of America, and on the Continent of Europe, stamp collecting forms a large branch of business; this study is pursued to an extent quite unknown here, and Philatelic Societies flourish in abundance. Hitherto the name of Sir Rowland Hill alone has been recognised as the inventor of the Adhesive Postage Stamp, or of the penny postage scheme itself; but from the evidence now adduced by me, these impressions have been widely admitted as having been a mistake, and the origin of the stamp transferred to James Chalmers. Nor has this transfer been confined to the Philatelic world. Historical Societies, University and State Libraries, with members of the Press having likewise admitted my claims.

THE UNITED STATES OF AMERICA.

To the 13 Philatelic Societies in the United States already mentioned, I am now enabled to add several others which have formally recognised James Chalmers as the inventor of the stamp, the various designs of which in all countries of the world it is the special object of the Philatelist to collect, and the list is now as under :—

The Chicago Philatelic Society	...	...	Chicago, Illinois.
The Pomeroy	,,	,,	... Toledo, Ohio.
The St. Louis	,,	,,	... St. Louis, Missouri.
The Lansing	,,	,,	... Lansing, Michigan.
The Newton	,,	,,	... Newtonville, Massachusetts.
The Jamestown	,,	,,	... Jamestown, New York.
The Charleston	,,	,,	... Charleston, South Carolina.
The Black Hawk	,,	,,	... Rock Island, Illinois.
The Belle City	,,	,,	... Racine, Wisconsin.
The Luther	,,	,,	... Luther, Michigan.
The Chalmers	,,	,,	... Chicago, Illinois.
The Salem	,,	,,	... Salem, Massachusetts.
The New Milford	,,	,,	... New Milford, Connecticut.
The Detroit	,,	,,	... Detroit, Michigan.
The Minneapolis	,,	,,	... Minneapolis, Minnesota.
The Rhode Island	,.	,,	... Providence, Rhode Island.
The Denver Stamp Collector's League ...	...	...	... Denver, Colorado.
Clan Cameron, No. 7, O.S.C.		...	... Providence, Rhode Island.
Grand Clan of Rhode Island, O.S.C. ...	...	...	... Providence, Rhode Island.

Ten of the above Societies have been good enough to elect me an honorary member, and several of the Philatelic journals have published a biographical sketch of James Chalmers, with portrait.

But the Philatelists of the United States, in addition to their local societies have formed themselves into one grand united body, termed the American Philatelic Association. This Association meets once a year, attracting members and delegates from all parts of the Union to enjoy a fortnight's discussion in support of their favourite pursuit. At the meeting held in Chicago, in August, 1887, the following resolutions were passed, with one dissentient :—

" Secretary's Office,
" Grand Crossing, Ill.,
" *September* 12*th*, 1887.

" Mr. Pat. Chalmers, London.

" Dear Sir,

" It is my pleasant task to inform you that at " the second Annual Convention of the American Philatelic " Association, held in Chicago, Ill., on August 8th, 9th, " and 10th, the following resolutions were adopted :—

" ' *Resolved :* That this Association, upon proof sub- " ' mitted by living witnesses, does endorse the claims " ' made by Mr. Patrick Chalmers on behalf of his father, " ' the late James Chalmers, as inventor of the Adhesive " ' Stamp; and be it further—

" ' *Resolved :* That the congratulations of this Associa- " ' tion be extended to Mr. Patrick Chalmers for the success " ' his untiring efforts have attained in establishing beyond " ' doubt an important historical fact; and be it still " ' further—

" ' *Resolved :* That the Secretary be instructed to for- " ' ward a copy of these resolutions to Mr. Patrick Chalmers, " ' and have the same published in the official journal.'

" With deep personal regard, I beg to remain,

" Yours very truly,
" S. B. BRADT,
" *Secretary American Philatelic Association.*"

To which Mr. Bradt added in a further kindly letter :—

" Accept my profound congratulations on the ever-increasing strength you are adding to your cause, and my best wishes for the speedy arrival of the time when its justice shall be universally conceded."

The meeting of this Association for 1888 took place at Boston, about which period, under date August 23rd, I was favoured with a letter of great ability on the whole subject from an esteemed correspondent, with permission to to quote same. This letter, of twelve pages, deals with two points ; first, with that of the Penny Postage Scheme itself, and next as regards the Stamp, with which latter question my present pages are concerned ; and it is with pleasure that I now quote the following :—

" I have now in my possession all the reports that bear " on this subject—5th, 9th, 1, 2 & 3 (of 1837-38) 1844, " 1858, &c., &c. I have seen and had copies made of Mr. " Rowland Hill's paper, ' On the collection of postage by " means of stamps,' the *Post Circular* containing your " father's proposals, and side by side with them a letter " from Sir Rowland Hill, ' The Life of Sir Rowland Hill,' " numerous other books on stamps, Stamp Acts, &c. I " have examined all that Hansard gives about stamps of " all kinds for a good many years, and things that have " not been alluded to in this discussion. I have quite a " pile of the original Acts of Parliament that bear on this " subject, and all this has taken up much time. So far " the investigation has not changed my mind, and justifies, " in my opinion, the position I have already assumed."

The writer then begins by dealing with the point as to the origin of the penny postage scheme and prior sources available to Mr. Hill for drawing up same ; and, continuing, "This brings me down to the second point—the use of stamps for collecting postage," touches upon the first traces of stamps, detached or impressed, in early times and occasionally, in England and elsewhere from 1653 to 1818, bringing the subject down to our modern practice and the question at issue :—

"When the agitation for a reduction of the taxes on
" knowledge began, Mr. Charles Whiting in 1830 (2nd
" Report, Select Committee of 1838-9, 11,253) proposed
" to separate the postal tax from the Excise tax, and to
" use covers or envelopes for such newspapers as passed
" the post, and suggested extending the use of such covers
" to letters in case the plan worked. There seems to have
" been no doubt about this. In 1834 Mr. Charles Knight
" (companion to newspaper) again suggested the use of
" stamped covers for newspapers. Mr. J. Chalmers at that
" time suggested, according to the recollection of certain
" old citizens * of Dundee, and actually had made
" Adhesive Stamps (for the same purpose perhaps), and
" advocated their use upon letters. Now, Mr. Rowland
" Hill admits that he got his idea of stamps for postage
" from Mr. Knight. If the fact be admitted that
" Mr. Chalmers did so propose and make adhesive stamps,
" can it be possible that, widely known as it was repre-
" sented to be, Mr. R. Hill did not get also his famous
" suggestion of a bit of gummed paper from the same
" source ? But Mr. Pearson Hill thinks the idea of sug-
" gesting the use of stamps for letters in 1834 was impro-
" bable or impracticable—let him say how it happened that
" Whiting *suggested it in* 1830 ? But up to 1834 we have
" not yet found any traces of the Adhesive Stamp.† Sir
" Rowland Hill says 'they were not thought of.' But
" Mr. Pearson Hill thinks ungummed medicine stamps
" were the same as adhesive—let father and son settle it
" between themselves. Mr. Pearson Hill says the idea of
" an adhesive stamp was 'certain to have occurred to
" scores of persons the moment the adoption of a uniform
" rate of postage, coupled with prepayment, rendered the

* Here I may be permitted to add, not only of citizens but of men then in his employment who took part in getting up the gummed sheets of stamps.

† I beg that this conclusive declaration may be noted.

" general use of stamps for postal purposes practicable '—
" will he explain why the idea of an adhesive stamp for
" revenue purposes did not occur to scores of people when
" the use of stamps for revenue purposes was not only
" practicable by imposition not only in England for many
" purposes which used detached stamps, but also in other
" countries? or why it should more easily suggest itself for
" postal purposes when it was to be applied to letters than
" when it was to be applied to newspaper wrappers? Ac-
" cording to Mr. Rowland Hill's first notion, it was to
" meet the contingency of a letter written and directed
" being brought by an ignorant person to the Post Office—
" would not the same thing be as likely to happen if the
" same ignorant person were going to send a newspaper?
" Trivial as the difference between a detached ungummed
" stamp and an adhesive stamp may seem now to Mr.
" Pearson Hill, others can readily see what would have
" been the fate of the thousands necessary for use if every
" person had had to resort to wafers, gum, or paste, in
" order to use them. The U.S. Patent Office, in 1861,
" thought the difference between a gummed wrapper and an
" ungummed one sufficient to entitle the former to a
" patent.

" It remains to be considered what does Mr. Pearson
" Hill's claim of priority of publication amount to. I
" am not sufficiently acquainted with English patent
" decisions to know what would be the decision in Eng-
" land, but I think the rule would require before the
" cases of the French and Italian systems could affect
" the question that they must have been published
" in a book actually or probably brought to England;
" and in the case that James Chalmers were shown to
" have actually made and distributed his Adhesive
" Stamp as is claimed, and the more so if he circulated a
" printed plan with them in 1834, the mere publication of
" Hill's idea in a pamphlet would not give him a priority
" over the man who had made and exhibited his invention
" which the pamphlet man would be supposed to know of.

" The rule has been stated by Mr. Hill as it applies to
" *discoveries*, not as I conceive it as applied to *inventions*.

" It is a universal rule of law, I conceive, that before
" you can invoke the testimony of part of a correspondence
" you must put in the whole, and you may further put in
" evidence any attendant circumstances which may serve
" to explain it. Until Mr. Pearson Hill consents to pro-
" duce the whole correspondence, he must not rely on the
" part he has chosen to quote. In fact, as it stands, it
" does not appear to me necessarily an acknowledgment
" that Hill was entitled to the claim. Had Chalmers
" wanted to have said, ' Notwithstanding all you have said,
" I am still the inventor, but you are in power and I must
" yield any way; and, as the public has got what I pro-
" posed to give them, I suppose I must be content,' he
" could hardly have chosen better, language to express the
" idea politely. Consequently it appears to me that the
" whole decision of this case depends on the credit to be
" given or refused to the Dundee witnesses—that Mr. Pear-
" son Hill has set up as barriers mere technicalities, which
" must go down before any fair investigator, in fact have
" no existence at all. . . . The Adhesive Stamp is as
" different from impressed stamps and detached stamps as
" covers are. Knight was the publisher of Hill's pamphlets,
" all editions, and one can hardly doubt that he knew of
" Chalmers' plan if it really was in existence before Hill's.*
" So that, after all, your father's case stands, as we said it
" did, on the evidence of the witnesses ; and while I did not
" draft or even suggest the resolutions, I suggested striking
" out some things to leave it where it is a year ago, and I

---

* In this connection it should be borne in mind that Mr. Rowland Hill, in
the *first* edition of his pamphlet, said nothing about the bit of gummed
paper—this allusion was only brought forward in the second edition—did
Mr. Hill *invent* the idea in the interval or was he put up to it? (See *ante*,
page 27.) An idea, moreover, of which he made no use until eighteen months
after Chalmers had officially proposed his plan. Thus, supposing for a moment
that Hill did invent this idea, and even Mr. Pearson Hill does not specially
claim this, it is still to Chalmers we are indebted for its application. But that
Chalmers was equally the inventor is proved by irrefragable evidence.

" stand by it now, and have ever since, and have no inten-
" tion of departing from it until something is brought
" forward that shakes that testimony.* There is a flaw
" in the evidence of one witness, but that does not shake
" the rest."

My Philadelphia friends will read the following with
interest :—

"320 s, 11th STREET, PHILADELPHIA,
"18th October, 1888.

" DEAR SIR,
" Your kind favour duly to hand. I cannot
understand the blindness of your adversaries for *res judi-
cata est*, and any further opposition can be only from
stupidity and obstinacy. I speak entirely without preju-
dice, and hope your filial efforts will be ultimately crowned
with the fullest success.

"Very respectfully yours,
"HENRY PHILLIPS, JUN.

" Mr. PATRICK CHALMERS,
"Wimbledon."

Dr. Phillips is author of numerous historical and practical works on Currency, &c., and has followed this controversy for years.

Many letters to similar effect continue to reach me;
but I now leave the United States and proceed to

PARIS.

Here the Société Internationale de Timbrologie, with
branches at Moscow, Odessa, and Stockholm, has passed
formal recognition in favour of James Chalmers as having
been the originator of the Adhesive Postage Stamp, and
has further been pleased to elect me an honorary member

* I may here point rather to the *additional* and confirmatory evidence in
the testimony of George Hood and Mr. Wears.

of the Society. The official journal of the Society, *L'Union des Timbrophiles*, having a circulation of 5,000 copies monthly, editor M. Nalés, has given a biographical sketch and portrait of James Chalmers, and has continued to publish matters of interest and progress on the subject as they arise.

The *Écho de la Timbrologie*, official journal of the Société Française de Timbrologie, published at Douai by Ed. Fremy Fils, has issued a series of articles in recognition of James Chalmers.

VIENNA.

Here I have been specially fortunate in having been favoured with the support of the keen Philatelist and able writer, Lieut.-Col. Charles Von Gündel, from whose pen has issued a translation, published in the *Postwertzeichen* of Munich, of Mr. Macintyre's article in the *Glasgow Magazine*; likewise a sharp criticism in the *Philatelischen Borsen-Courier*, of an article which lately appeared in the *Liverpool Daily Post*, in which article that eminent paper, while giving up Rowland Hill, could not recognise Chalmers who had never asserted himself or been before heard of. (This, it will be seen, is a mistake.) Col. Von Gündel has likewise contributed many articles in favour of James Chalmers to the German Philatelic journals, giving an account of the Penny Postal Reform and the services of Chalmers in having initiated the stamp which saved it. Von Gündel has further contributed to the *Wiener Briefmarken Zeitung* an able criticism of the late pamphlet of Mr. Pearson Hill, in which article the fallacies contained in that pamphlet are exposed, and the allegations dealt with *seriatim*, and effectually answered.

The same Vienna journal, editor H. Koch, has published articles in recognition of Chalmers.

The *Welt Post*, conducted by Herr Sigmund Friedl, proprietor of the extensive International Stamp Museum, Unter-Döbling, Vienna, has afforded me warm support, and has published a biographical sketch of James Chalmers, with portrait.

The *Neues Wiener Tagblatt*, in lately noticing the remarkable museum of Herr Friedl at Unter-Döbling, remarks :—

" Portraits, pamphlets, and similar matter, remind us
" that the Postage Stamp introduced in 1839 by Rowland
" Hill, of the English Post Office, is not considered as his
" creation, but as that of James Chalmers, a printer, of
" Dundee. We see the first English stamp—a most won-
" derful sight ! We need not be surprised did the Imperial
" German Postal Museum possess one, since there the
" Museum is maintained by the State, but the institution
" in Döbling owes its establishment to the exertions of a
" private individual."

BERLIN.

Here James Chalmers has been formally recognised by the Berlin Philatelic Club, and an article in two numbers, descriptive of his services, has appeared in the *Mittheilungen des Berliner Phil. Club*, the journal of the Society.

In *Der Sammler*, " organ der Berliner Briefmarken-Borse, and der Vereins der Briefmarken Sammler zu Berlin," published and edited by Dr. Brendicke, has appeared an excellent likeness and biographical notice of James Chalmers.

It is further with no small satisfaction that I present the following translation from the *Deutsche Verkehrs Zeitung*, or German Traffic Journal, " organ of the General Post Office and Telegraphic Affairs, and their officials," of Berlin, August 31st, 1888 :—

" Until a short time ago Sir Rowland Hill, the late British Post Office Secretary, known through his reforms in Postal matters, has been looked upon as the inventor of the Adhesive Postage Stamp. However, lately, only through careful investigations, it has been ascertained that this service is due to the bookseller, James Chalmers, of Dundee, who died in 1853.

" Chalmers' carefully worked-out ideas and plans were laid before the British Treasury, and his system of the Adhesive Postage Stamp was adopted by Treasury Minute of the 26th December, 1839. At that time Rowland Hill was an official of the British Treasury.

" On the 6th May, 1840, namely forty-eight years ago, the first issue of Adhesive Postage Stamps appeared in England."

The article goes on to notice the periods at which other nations adopted " the indispensable invention of Chalmers, until such had been adopted by all the countries of the globe as time passed on."

The above article has been reproduced by such leading German papers as the *Frankfort Gazette*, and others. Same has appeared in the original German in the *Londoner Zeitung*, circulating amongst the German community in this country.

LEIPZIG.

In this Philatelic stronghold my success has been very marked. In the first place, the *Illustrirtes Briefmarken Journal*, the organ of thirty-three Philatelic Societies, published by Gebruders Senf, and having a bi-monthly circulation of 12,000 copies, has recognised and written about the services of James Chalmers in four articles continued in nine numbers of the issue. On the frontispiece of this important journal appears the head of James Chalmers in conjunction with that of Sir Rowland Hill.

Very important too is the accession of the learned Dr. Moschkau, the friend and correspondent of Sir Rowland Hill, to the ranks of those who recognise James Chalmers, as may be read in the following extract from his journal, the *Illustrirte Briefmarken Zeitung* of August 15th, 1888 :—

" To a correspondent who asks ' Which view does the editor of this paper take concerning the affair Hill-Chalmers so frequently referred to lately?' the learned Dr. Moschkau replies :—

" ' How could we do otherwise than believe that Chalmers is in the right! We have had personally some correspondence with Sir R. Hill a short time before his death, and we propose to refer to same some time later on in this paper.' "

Subsequently, several articles, in six numbers, from the pen of Col. Von Gündel, descriptive of the Penny Postage Reform and the services of James Chalmers have, with the sanction and assent of Dr. Moschkau, appeared in his journal, the organ of several societies. I regret that space compels me for the present to withhold translations of these able contributions.

FRANKFORT.

Here the large and important Philatelic Society, the Verein für Briefmarken, Herr Albert Schindler, Secretary, has formally recognised James Chalmers; the *Illustrirte Frankfürter Briefmarken Zeitung Universum*, editor H. J. Dauth, has published throughout eight numbers a long article having reference to the services of Chalmers.

DRESDEN.

The *Deutsche Briefmarken Zeitung*, edited by Herr E. W. Grossman, Secretary to the Dresden Philatelic Verein (not the Internationaler Society) has published two articles in recognition of Chalmers.

MUNICH.

In the *Mittheilungen des Bayarischen Philatelisten Vereins*, the official journal of the large Bavarian Philatelic Society, Herr Anton Bachl, the Secretary, has produced two articles on the fresh light I have thrown as to the origin of the adhesive stamp. Other articles in recognition of Chalmers have appeared in *Das Postwerthzeichen*, editor Th. Hass.

MARISCH-AUSTRIA.

The *Philatelischer Borsen-Courier*, editor Herr C. C. Sauer, has published three articles in support of my cause, including the criticism already mentioned under the heading of "Vienna" upon the article in the *Liverpool Daily Post*.

CZERNOWITZ-AUSTRIA.

The Czernowitz Philatelic Society *Orient* has formally recognised James Chalmers. To Herr Mittelmann, of this Society, my special thanks are due for much appreciated correspondence and warm support.

STOCKHOLM.

In the *Tedning für Frimerkamlare*, the editor, M. R. J. Bruzelins, has published an account of the services of James Chalmers as originator of the adhesive stamp, with portrait.

CONSTANTINOPLE.

An excellent Philatelic journal published here in the French language, *Le Timbre Levantin*, editor-in-chief M. Hissard, has a wide circulation throughout the Levant and elsewhere. In this able paper lengthened articles have appeared in vindication of the services of James Chalmers ; and to its editor and conductors, M. M. I. Tchakidji et Cie, I am under great obligations.

CONCLUSION.

It is thus seen that, *where attention has been given* to this matter of national and historical interest, an impartial perusal of my publications has resulted in something like a unanimous verdict that James Chalmers was the originator of the Adhesive Postage stamp, a verdict which his countrymen will receive and respond to with something more than satisfaction. That my list of Continental recognitions does not include the entire Philatelic body is much owing, as I am informed by some of the heads of these Societies, to the difference of language preventing their members at large from grasping the facts of the case so as to overcome long-cherished delusions. The same may be said with respect to many editors, literary men, and others here, too prejudiced even to *read* what has been published, with many important cases of which nature I am well acquainted.

PATRICK CHALMERS, *F.R.Hist.Soc.*,

Honorary Member of the Société Internationale de Timbrologie, Paris, and of Ten American Philatelic Societies.

WIMBLEDON,
    January, 1889.

POSTSCRIPT.

Having just been informed that statements have been circulated in the United States, said to have emanated from Mr. Pearson Hill, that the Treasury Minute Extract of date 11th March, 1864, given at page 13 herewith, was subsequently withdrawn by the Treasury; and further, that the Resolution of the Town Council of Dundee, of date 3rd March, 1883, in favour of James Chalmers, was subsequently withdrawn by that Town Council—matters which I am charged with having suppressed in my publications—I beg to make known that such statements are wholly without foundation and contrary to the facts.

That the words in the Treasury Minute, printed in italics at page 13, were at any time withdrawn is a mere assertion, no proof of which has been or can be produced. On the contrary, when, in the following June, the proposal to grant the sum of £20,000 to Sir Rowland Hill for his services was brought forward in Parliament, the very occasion to make the correction and the *amende* if due, neither

Lord Palmerston in the Commons nor Lord Granville in the Lords for one moment admitted any mistake whatever in the terms of that Treasury Minute. So far from doing so, Lord Granville indorses the terms of that Minute (see *Hansard*, June, 1864). It was for his *services*, not as having been an inventor, that the recompense was given.

With respect to the Dundee Town Council Resolution of 3rd March, 1883, the official notification of which from the Town Clerk is now before me, so far from such having at any time been withdrawn as .stated, the same was actually repeated and confirmed upon the occasion of my having applied to erect a memorial to James Chalmers, recording him as " having been the originator of the Adhesive Postage Stamp," the official notification of which permission from the Town Clerk, of date 11th April, 1888, is also now before me.

It is consequently not true that I have suppressed anything with reference to these or any other matters ; and I can only caution the Philatelic world and my readers against entertaining statements of this nature, and there may be others such which I have not seen, put forward for the mere purpose of endeavouring to discredit me by opponents who have no case of their own.

P. C.

Wimbledon,
    February, 1889.

Effingham Wilson & Co., Printers, Royal Exchange, E.C.